Table of contents

Dedication

Introduction

Basic interior design principles

Different interior design styles

How to keep home makeovers within your budget

50 Interior design tips for beginners

Conclusion

_____

Dedication

This book is dedicated to all my readers who want to decorate their homes, to those who want to free up space and want to learn about interior design. I believe that you can achieve this, because I have. And if I can do that, you can do that, too. I believe in you!

Introduction

You might need to do some redecorating if you recently moved into a new place or if you just want to spruce the one you live in. As you are aware, it can be quite challenging to redecorate because it takes up a lot of thought, time, effort, and money, but in the end, it is all worth it. This guide will help you redecorate your home in a hassle free way that will surely not put a dent in your budget.

Basic interior design principles

Before you can redecorate any space, you must have some basic knowledge of interior design principles. When you get into some well designed rooms, you get a feeling that everything in it is just right and cohesive. You can achieve the same effect in your own home or the space you are decorating by having some knowledge of those principles. Some of them include:

Balance:

In the art of design, balance is essential as it brings out a feeling of equilibrium. Balance involves approximating or equalizing the weight of objects (visual). Balance is created when you are able to equalize colors, shapes, texture, and patterns. There are various kinds of balance:

Formal or symmetrical balance:

Formal or traditional rooms/spaces require you to balance symmetrically. In this kind of balance, the space is split evenly in two portions that mirror each other. For instance, you can put two chairs on each side of a dining/coffee table to achieve symmetrical balance. This balance is easy to attain as the elements of design are repeated on each of the two portions. However, if not properly used, this balance can end up being boring and monotonous.

Informal or asymmetrical balance:

In this kind of balance, the visual weight of colors, lines, textures, and forms are balanced individually without duplication. Informal balance is not as ordered as formal balance and can be more interesting and complex. For example, a couch can be balanced by putting two chairs on either of its sides.

Radial balance: This balance is attained when there is a focal point in the centre from which other objects radiate from or around. A good example of such an arrangement would be a round table, with chairs (preferably same design) well arranged around it. Here, there is a lot of repetition of color texture and form.

Rhythm

Rhythm focuses on creating a pattern of contrast and repetition to create visual interest. This can be attained by using the same shape or color at equal/different intervals. The purpose of this principle is to make someone move their eyes around the room. You can achieve this by creating a pattern using a common colors in pillows, continuing it in a painting, and picking it up again in a rug. These repetitions will make the observer's eye be carried around the room.

Harmony

Harmony is brought up when all elements in the room combine to create a common message. Harmony in the elements of a room bring about a feeling of restfulness. For example, you can bring about harmony by use of just one color. You can do this even though your forms greatly vary in size, texture, and shape.

Emphasis

If everything gets equal attention in your room, it may become boring or scattered. You need to look for an anchor. Many rooms often have a built in point of interest like a window with a beautiful view or a fireplace. You can decide to enhance that point by maybe arranging some furniture around it, to put an emphasis on it. If your room lacks such a point, you can create your own by using a large or unusual piece of furniture or grouping the furniture in one place.

Proportion and scale

Proportion is the ratio of size between two parts. The scale in this comparison, is how the size of an object relates to another or placement of the object in the room. For example, if you create an overstuffed section in a small room, it would be out of scale. Some proportions are rather more pleasing than others. The early Greeks created the "Golden Section", aimed to summarize all proportion to a simple formula: The ratio of the smaller section should equate to that of the larger section to the entire space.

Now that you are aware of the basic principles of interior design, let us move on to various interior design styles.

Different interior design styles

Before you begin your project, you should be able to understand that there are different kinds of designs you can use to redecorate your house to suite your taste.

Modern

This style was created by a group of European designers, which started at the Bauhaus School of Design (Germany) in 1919. The philosophy of Bauhaus is that function and form should mix all designs. This style is clean-lined and firstly focuses on function avoiding excessive decorative elements and accessories. Some people can consider modern design to be harsh, cold, or too simple, but if it is well planned, it can create a sense of calmness and simplicity in your house. This style is best used for small spaces and apartments as it makes the room seem larger than it is.

Contemporary

This one uses trendy looks that are currently in style. Contemporary style creates welcoming and comfortable interiors without being dark and cluttered. It is suitable for stores, homes, lofts, and offices. It uses bold color blocks, square-edged furniture, high ceilings, floor mats, linear wooden floors, geometric shapes, and bare windows.

Minimalist

Minimalist became widely used in the late 1980's New York and London. This design uses simplicity and cold blue or white lighting with white elements, and large spaces with minimum furniture and objects. As natural light flows in a space with minimalist interior design, it reveals clean and simple spaces.

Classic

Classic style is based on order, balance, and symmetry. They key element in this style is use of a central/focal point around which balance (visual) is achieved. The color theme in classic style is inspired by nature. They include shades of green, yellow, brown, and blue. The fabrics used tend to be elegant without being attention grabbing. Velvet, canvas, and cotton are commonly used. Flooring is mostly of marble, stone, or wood. Classic style uses formal balance of interior design as mentioned earlier.

Urban

The design features and materials used in this style are non-traditional. Galvanized steel, metal siding, concrete floors, unfinished surfaces, and exposed beams are used in this style. Often, random objects are used in interiors with urban style to create an industrial or outdoor atmosphere. The look is polished further with sophisticated finishes, bespoke fixtures, and small, clever space use.

Country

Country is comfortable and it resembles cottage style. There are different country style types, depending on the country of origin such as the French style, English style, Italian style, and American style. The country style makes use of the features from the culture of the country from which it originates.

Art deco

This style came up after World War I, aiming to bring people a new era style. The furniture in art deco style is streamlined, design wise. This design is sleek and modern, being comfortable at the same time. Most color schemes in this style include black mixed with other colors such as red, green, or white while chrome and gold are used as accent colors. For a softening effect, dove gray and pale blue are used. This style also makes use of extensive lighting including floor lamps, wall lamps, ceiling lights, and table lamps. Most of these lights are usually warm (yellow or orange in color). The surfaces in Art Deco Style are clean and sleek, lacking any texture. This style was used to show off prosperity and renewed wealth after World War I.

Retro

After a few decades, some old designs seem to be brought up again but with a modern touch. Retro style uses that mixture of modern and old styles. This style relies on your past, as there are too many styles to choose from. This makes this style hard to recognize as it varies. The only feature that can help you point it out is the combination of modern and old styles.

Rococo

Rococo is rich and flamboyant with ornate and intricate features. It became popular during the 1700 and 1780 around Western Europe. One of the key features of this style is gold plaster work. Mirrors are also used in Rococo styles, which are shaped intricately with gilded frames.

The furniture used in this style is made of mahogany and upholstered in velour, brocade, or leather. It also comprises of sinuous and carved silhouettes that complement the ceiling and wall finishing. Colors used in this Rococo style include pink, yellow, gold, ivory, cream, and azure blue.

Georgian

Previously, Georgian style was from Queen Anne Design and gradually became popular in architectural detail. The color schemes used included dusky rose, sage, powder blue, pea green, and subtle blue. This style uses delicate furniture, and the design brings out a royal feel.

Victorian

This style was created during the Victorian era. It is often described as opulent and full of luxury. You can compare it to the near opposite of minimalism style. The Victorian style has its base on excessive amount of flamboyant decorations, accessories, and the ornate. Plain wall surfaces and floors contrast the excessive decorations. The Victorian style makes use of pastels and neutral colors.

With knowledge on the various design styles, let us now look at the various colors and how to choose a suitable color for your house.

Choosing room colors for your home

Choosing colors for each room in your home can be very hard. You can make this easier by first understanding colors and their effects on a room. You should keep in mind that colors tend to behave in three basic ways, namely passive, neutral, and active. You can pick a color for the different rooms according to the purpose of the room and taste. Brighter colors often make a room look bigger and brighter while darker colors bring a sense of warmness and sophistication. Dark colors can also give a room a more intimate appearance.

Some of the considerations you should make when choosing a color scheme for a room include :

-The purpose of the room (work, sleeping, relaxation, socializing)

- The people who will use the room most (kids/adults)

- Time of the day when the room will be used

- The amount of natural light that enters the room

- The colors of furniture that you will put in the room

-The mood and feelings you want each room to convey

Below are some colors, their effects on moods, and the best rooms to use them to decorate with:

Red: Red raises the energy level in a room. It is a good option when you want to create excitement, mostly at night. You can use a red color theme in your dining or living room to stimulate conversation and draw people together. Red has also been shown to speed up the heart rate, raise blood pressure, and increase respiration.

Yellow: Yellow communicates happiness and brings the joy of sunshine inside. It is good for dining rooms, bathrooms, and kitchens. It also brings about a welcoming feeling. Although yellow is a color that brings cheerfulness, it is not a good choice to use in designing rooms as a main color scheme. Some studies show that some people can actually lose their temper in rooms with yellow interiors. Additionally, in a yellow room, babies seem to cry more than usual.

Blue: This color has been said to slow heart rate, reduce respiration, and bring down blood pressure. It is considered to be relaxing, serene, and calming. It is recommended to be used in bathrooms and bedrooms. When used in a room that receives little or no natural light, some shades of blue (light shades) can bring out an unpleasant chilly feeling. However, if you want to use light blue as the main color in a room, use furnishings and fabrics that have warmer colors. Blue can also be used to enhance relaxation in rooms with a lot of social activity such as the living room. Do not use darker shades of blue as they may bring the opposite effect, bringing about feelings of sadness.

Green: Green is considered as a color that causes restfulness to the eye. It can be used in the kitchen to cool things down. It can also be used in a living room or family room to bring warmth and promote togetherness and comfort. Green is believed to relieve stress by creating a calming effect. It is also said to assist with fertility, thus making it a good option for the bedroom.

Purple: This color is believed to portray drama, sophistication, and richness. It is often linked to creativity, as an accent or luxury. As a secondary color, it gives the main color scheme depth. Lighter shades of purple, such as lilac and lavender, bring the same feeling of restfulness as blue, but without the chance of a chilly feeling.

Orange: This color evokes a feeling of enthusiasm and excitement and is an energetic color. It also brings out all the emotions you need to release during your fitness routine. In the ancient times, orange was believed to have a healing effect on the lungs and cause an increase in energy levels.

Neutrals (gray, white, brown, and black): These colors are highly flexible and always fall in and out of fashion. Black is used best as an accent with other colors.

Crimson: This color makes some people feel very irritated. It can also bring about feelings of hostility and rage. Thus, you should avoid using it as the main color scheme of a room.

When decorating, you should also consider your ceiling because it accounts for one-sixth of the space in your room. Mostly, white is used for ceilings. White has been considered the best choice for ceiling because it makes the ceiling feel higher.

A combination of blue, yellow, and green fits any room in the house because it combines all qualities of refreshing, cheerfulness, and calmness.

Enjoying this book so far? I'd love it for you to share your thoughts and post a quick review on Amazon!

Click here to leave a review on Amazon.com

How to keep home makeovers within your budget

I am sure with all the information on redecorating, you are wondering how you are going to keep that makeover within your budget. You don't have to worry though because there are many options that can help you reduce that big budget to something that is pocket friendly. Below are ways that you can reduce your budget:

Go online

The Internet offers a wide variety of websites in which you can either sell or buy items for very low prices. This comes in handy in your case because you can be able to sell some of those things in your home you don't need to create room for redecoration and also buy some other items on the same websites. Other online shopping websites also allow you to trade in what you have with other people without using any money. Some of these websites include: ebay.com , shopgoodwill.com , craigslist.org , thegreenumbrella.org , and ireuse.com, just to mention a few.

Do it yourself

You can easily renovate your home because hiring a professional can be quite expensive. However, before you can do the redecorations, it is important that you have some basic knowledge about interior design. You can go online and read the various resources on redecorating so that you can have all the information you need. You don't want to do something only for it to cost money and having to hire a professional anyway, which leads to more costs.

Shop at secondhand stores

You could try shopping at consignment stores, garage sales, thrift stores, estate sales, yard sales, and church rummage sales, which all offer great discounts on decoration items .

Bring in friends and family to your project

If you don't know a lot about redecoration of homes, you may call in some of your friends, family, and neighbors to assist you get your home redecoration project off the ground. These people will supply you with the muscle you need to move things around, paint, or even rip wall paneling down. Just don't forget to provide lunch!

Opt for stock items

Stick to off-the-shelf items, which are often already made, instead of ordering custom items, which may make you spend more. We all know that custom items/designer can be worth big bucks.

Be patient and wait for discounts

Many stores offer high discounts during certain times, especially during holiday seasons such as Christmas. You can wait for these times and get your decoration items at a lower price. As you shop, you can ask department and store managers when some of the items you need will be on discount.

Re-use some of the items you have

You don't have to throw away the items you already have when you redecorate your house. For example, if your couch is old and the fabrics are torn and full of stains, you can renovate it by removing the old fabric and going for other covers that suit your taste and fix them on the couch. Not only will it have a new look, but it will have a unique design. You can also re-paint some of the furniture in your house to give it a new look.

Sew your own linens

If you have a sewing machine at home, you can easily and quickly transform your old sheets into pillow duvet covers, pillow covers, and curtain panels.

Mix

Trying to match up everything in your home can sometimes look boring. Buying full sets of couches and other furniture can be very costly; instead, go for a mixed style, which is rather cheap and gives the house an electric look. Don't feel shy to combine traditional and modern or low-end and high-end as the result will be unique and beautiful as well.

Let us look at some amazing interior design tips that will be of great help when you try to decorate your home.

50 Interior design tips for beginners

1. *Follow the current trends in changeable ways.* You can add some accessories such as pillows, rugs, and lamps. This will make your home look as if it has changed with current trends. This method is budget friendly and enables you to stay up-to-date easily.

2. *Add some color to the stair risers of your staircase to liven it up.* Choose a color that is contemporary to your walls or even cover them with an exciting wall covering. You can also paint them in an ombre pattern with a color from your home's story, if you are adventurous. This change is small but brings out a large impact.

3. *For a small space, dominate white.* White is a color that, even when used in small spaces, tends to make the space larger. This is your best option when painting a small room.

4. *Remember your dining chairs.* You can add pillows on your dining chairs, which are an easy way to make your dining more intimate. You can even go to the extent of replacing the chairs with pillows that are designed especially for that in the market today.

5. *Don't waste time hunting for vintage cabinets.* Instead of looking for old cabinets, which may be hard to find and expensive, to give your home a classic feel, build your own by using old glass doors and windows in your home.

6. *To give personality to your rooms, use area rugs.* On hard surfaces, you can make use of rugs to reduce echo and provide comfort. The area rug defines the room with pattern, texture, and color beautifully.

7. *Use a vintage look by applying a vintage frame on a standard mirror.* Use 1 by 3 inch pine strips, paint them same color as your walls and soften them at the edges. You can also add depth and interest to a dull wall by placing rectangular boards around fixtures and mirrors. The look is subtle as well as

effective.

8. *Use pillows that contrast in color on the back and front.* This can be used to bring a small change to appearance as you flip them from time to time.

9. *Add a dramatically patterned chair.* You can add this chair to your living room or a pair in your dining room, which will capture the eye.

10. *Establish the right focal point.* This is one of the key principles that can change the appearance of your room greatly. The most visible focal points are in built features of the room/house such as the fireplace or window. If your room does not have one, you can create it yourself with use of a unique furniture piece or a good piece of artwork.

11. *Every room needs three things.* There are some things that you should not miss in each room to enhance appearance such as candles, flowers, and mirrors.

12. *Use nice plates and platters to enhance color in your rooms.* When you hang small groupings of different plate sizes on your wall or even place them on bookshelves or plate stands, a beautiful pattern is formed, bringing color to your room. These plates can be easily found in flea markets and are a cheap way to increase interest to a space.

13. *Think of waterfalls when you are working with accessories.* As you accessorize your house, start with the biggest things at the back and flow down from there. Nothing gets lost that way.

14. *Make use of crisp linens and fresh flowers to also enhance color in your space/room.*

15. *Remember to layer light.* There are three types of lighting you can use: task, ambient, and accent. All these types of lighting should be present for the best effect in your rooms.

16. *Start redesigning your room with something you really love.* This may be

a painting, a rug, or anything. This way, you can be able to set the color and style and have a baseline of the design to start re-decorating.

17. *Keep in mind that collaborative design brings out the best.* If you are not good at designing, you can get in contact with a designer before you consult a contractor.

18. *The art of lighting correctly brings the room to life.* Correct lighting also makes your room/space sparkle. The correct light must be placed at the right angle and distance, according to height and size of the room and how art is placed on the walls.

19. *Don't forget the guest bathroom.* Hang important art in there. It will capture the attention of your guests. Don't forget to put everything that the guest might need in the bathroom.

20. *Make use of reflective materials.* Use objects that reflect light such as chandeliers, mirrors, and other elements made of glass that have qualities that open up a room, bringing a touch of glamour.

21. *If you are not sure what end table or sofa size to purchase, lay big bags on the floor in the room you want to set.* This way, you will be able to see what works best in terms of placement and size. It helps you to visualize the place before purchasing an item that is either too small or too big.

22. *Raise your eyes.* Before you hang wallpaper on the wall, try different points of the rooms, even on the ceiling as long as it is not heavy. If you use regular wallpapers that have organic texture or little shimmer, you will give a boring ceiling an elegant designer look.

23. *Buy a great sofa.* Buy a set that will suit your needs and bring easiness to the room.

24. *Choose the right kind of chairs.* It is recommended that you try to look for more comfortable, stylish, and timeless chairs than the common French bergères.

25. *Don't choose pieces that are too small for your room.* Look for elements that will suit the size of your room. Don't go for big items when your room is small or vice versa to avoid imbalance in sections.

26. *Try original artwork.* Some people tend to fear looking for original artwork because they have a mentality that it is expensive. Students and local artists provide artwork at cheaper prices. You can even create some artwork yourself if you have an artistic side.

27. *Try looking for vintage items from thrift stores.* This will give your home a unique look.

28. *Make use of flowers.* You should try to put something organic in every room in your house. Use unique containers for preserved or real flowers such as teapots, wine bottles, and even milk jugs. Flowers bring a colorful look to your house.

29. *Make your bedroom your sanctuary.* The first thing that obviously comes to your mind is to get the computer and TV out the bedroom. Your bedroom is the only place you can escape from all bad news and relax. So as you re-design it, ensure you put in everything that will help you relax during stressful times.

30. *Consult an expert interior designer.* Just as you would go for a pedicure or a manicure, hire an interior designer for a one-hour consultation. It will be money well spent on your home improvement in terms of interior design.

31. *Create playful shadows and ambience effect on walls.* This can be done by placing an up light in a corner just beneath a banana palm or fiddle-leaf fig.

32. *Backlighting for glass sinks.* Adding some back light to sinks made of glass results in a beautiful glow as well as creating a night light for your bathroom.

33. *Hang mirrors in correct positions.* Before you hang a mirror, look around

the room. A mirror can reflect things on the opposite side that may be rather embarrassing such as a hole in the wall or even dirty dishes from the position you put it.

34. *Drapery*. Always hang it at least eight to ten inches over the window molding. This makes the window look generally larger and taller. The same effect is brought with a shaped upholstered cornice.

35. *Reprint some of the colored family photos in black-and-white*. This is done to group them and make them uniform.

36. *Tight spaces*. If you have a small space in your room that needs to be filled but it isn't big enough to fit any furniture, you can place a mirror on the wall in that area. This makes the space nearly invisible.

37. *Put a lamp on the countertop*. Put it preferably in the bathroom for a feeling of intimacy and warmth.

38. *Get new lampshades*. To make a traditional lamp a little more modern, use a drum shade.

39. Use towels with monograms for bathrooms. This makes them look a little bit custom made. You can also add colorful soaps, lotions, and guest napkins that will enhance the visual appearance of the room.

40. *Painting a room*. For best results, when painting a room, you should use a "blush color" on the trim, ceiling, and doors. A blush color is a mixture of white and a touch of the color of your wall. The resulting effect pulls the room together.

41. *Make a decorative pillow*. You can add some color to the room by using unexpected found materials.

42. *As you design the room, consider the focal point, function, and flow*. First, figure out what you want to use the room for. Give purpose to the space then later create a focal point. Last, create a flow, ensuring you arrange the large

elements in your room so they face your focal point.

43. *Get the height right.* Hang a chandelier in your dining room approximately 36 inches above the table. For artwork, you should hang them between 60 to 65 inches from the centre to the floor. It doesn't matter how high your ceiling is.

44. *Use current color trends.* Currently, there's a shift from brown color shades to more grayish and blue shades. This color trend is approximated to go on for the next 10 years or so. If you are redecorating now, this would be the best color scheme for you to use to avoid an outdated look in the five years.

45. *Make paint the last of your choices to make.* There are many hundreds of thousands of paint colors you can choose from. This will obviously make it a tough decision to make. Start your redecoration project with processes that don't require you to make many choices such as cabinets, upholstery fabrics, and rugs, then move onto the walls. This will lay the foundation to the color that will be a more appropriate paint color to be used on the house.

46. *Working with accent colors.* Add them to the room in multiples of three (doesn't have to be of the same scale). For example, you can add an orange pillow, orange painting, and a small orange tray to a living room.

47. *The most inexpensive and quickest way to change a look is to fit new hardware on kitchen and bathroom cabinets.*

48. *Reupholstering just a single piece.* This can change the appearance of your room to a great extent.

49. *Improper use of family photos.* Family photos should not be taken as art and hung everywhere in the house, especially in prominent spots or in public areas. Opt to put them in more private places instead, where only the family can appreciate them. You can occasionally frame a group of photos and place them on top of a piano or table.

50. *Create a sense of formality.* You can do this by angling a few of your furniture pieces or even add artwork, mirrors or even accessories. This brings out the personality of the room.

Conclusion

Interior design can be very challenging to undertake at first, but once the project is off the ground, everything will fall into place. It just takes patience and will, and the end result will prove to be pretty worth it. All you need to do is to start somewhere and you will be amazed at how much you will achieve with this kind of attitude.

Thank you for downloading this book!

www.ingramcontent.com/pod-product-compliance
Lightning Source LLC
LaVergne TN
LVHW040755211224
799664LV00009B/382